EASTER JOKES FOR KIDS

D0169794

FROM _____

Q: What happens if you pour hot water down a big rabbit hole?

A: You get very Hot cross bunnies!

Q: What does the Easter bunny wear to look cool?

A: A 14 carrot gold necklace!

Q: What do you name a stinky rabbit with lots of ticks and lice?

A: Bugs Bunny!

Where does an Easter bunny go on holiday?

A: Easter islands

Q: Why is it a bad idea to tell a joke to an Easter egg?

A: Because it could crack up!

Q: How do you confuse the Easter bunny?

A: Tell him all the chocolate eggs have hatched

Q: What advice did the Easter egg give the hopeful boy?

A: Don't put all your eggs in one basket

Q: What did the hungry Easter bunny say?

A: I carrot wait for Easter!

Q: What can you give a very wet rabbit?

A: A hare-dryer of course!

Q: Where is the last place you would find Easter eggs?

A: In the toilet

Q: Why did the Angry Easter Bunny decide to cross the road?

A: Because the naughty chicken had all his Easter eggs!

Q: What did the hungry Easter rabbit say to the tasty carrot?

A: Nothing, rabbits can't talk!

Q: What's the worst thing about Easter egg hunting?

A: Getting chased by confused chickens

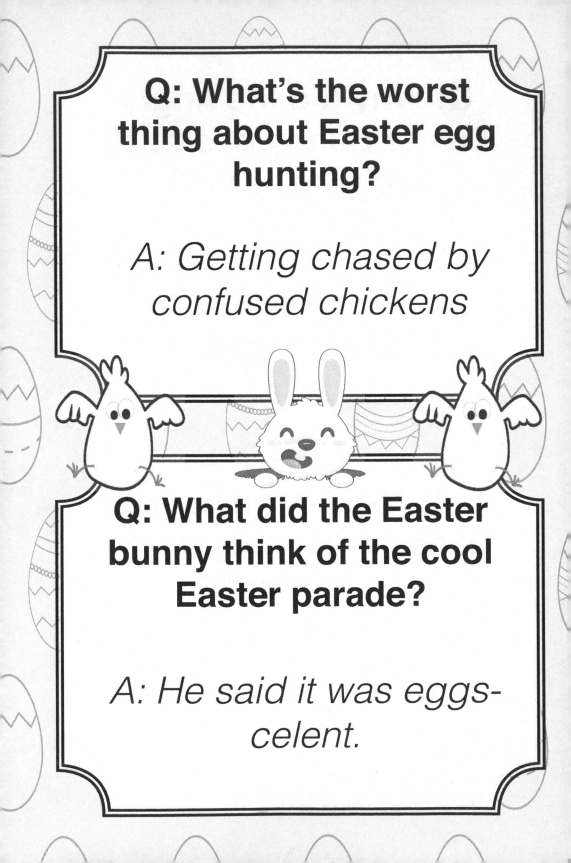

Q: What did the Easter bunny think of the cool Easter parade?

A: He said it was eggs-celent.

Q: How does the Easter bunny like to travel around the world?

A: On a deluxe Hare plane

Q: How does the healthy Easter Bunny stay so well?

A: He does a lot of eggs-ercise!

Q: Why did the little egg not want to play a game of hide and seek?

A: Because he was a little chicken!

Q: Did you know about the Easter Bunny that fell in love with a regular bunny?

A: They got married and lived hoppily ever after!

Q: Why do we hide eggs on Easter?

A: So chickens can't find them and sit on them

Q: Did you hear about the angry Easter bunny?

A: He was hopping mad

Q: Did you hear about the rabbit comedian?

A: He was a funny bunny!

Q: Did you hear about the recently married rabbits?

A: They have gone on their bunnymoon!

Q: How do you know that carrots are really good for your eyesight?

A: Well, have you ever seen rabbits hopping around wearing glasses?

Q: How do Easter rabbits collect their eggs?

A: They get them from an eggplant!

Q: Why do we usually paint regular Easter eggs?

A: Because we can't wallpaper them!

Q: Did you hear that once they crossed a rabbit with a bumblebee?

A: It's now a honey bunny!

Q: Why does the Easter bunny always have such clean fur?

A: Because he uses a hare brush!

Q: Did you hear there was an Easter bunny comedian?

A: He knew good yolks

Q: Do you know what the Easter bunny's favorite type of music is?

A: Hip hop!

Q: How do you know if the Easter bunny has been around?

A: Because Eggs mark the spot!

Q: Why should you never tickle an egg?

A: In case it cracks up

Q: What's a sick Easter bunny called with a blocked nose?

A: A runny bunny, of course!

Q: What is the Easter rabbit's favorite dance style?

A: The bunny hop!

Q: What stories do the Easter bunny enjoy?

A: Any with hoppy endings!

Q: Did you know once there was a rabbit that crossed with an insect?

A: He was known as Bugs Bunny!

Q: Did you hear about the Easter rabbit who couldn't find her comb?

A: She was so upset about having a bad hair day!

Q: Did you hear about the very naughty Easter bunny at school?

A: He was eggs-spelled.

Q: Why is there no Easter chickens?

A: Because they would sit on the eggs instead of hiding them

Q: Why is there no Easter monkeys?

A: because they would throw the eggs at you

Q: Why is there no Easter parrots?

A: Because they will tell you where the eggs are hidden

Q: Why are there no Easter tortoises?

A: They would take forever to hide the eggs

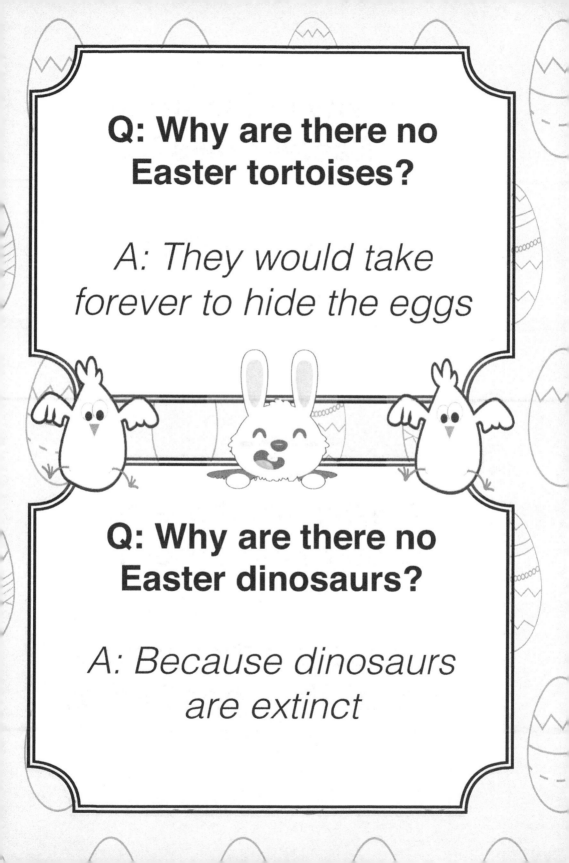

Q: Why are there no Easter dinosaurs?

A: Because dinosaurs are extinct

Q: Why are there no Easter cows?

A: Because they moooove too slow.

Q: Why are there no Easter kangaroos?

A: Because they would carry all the eggs in their pouch

Q: What is the Easter rabbit's favorite sport?

A:Basket-ball

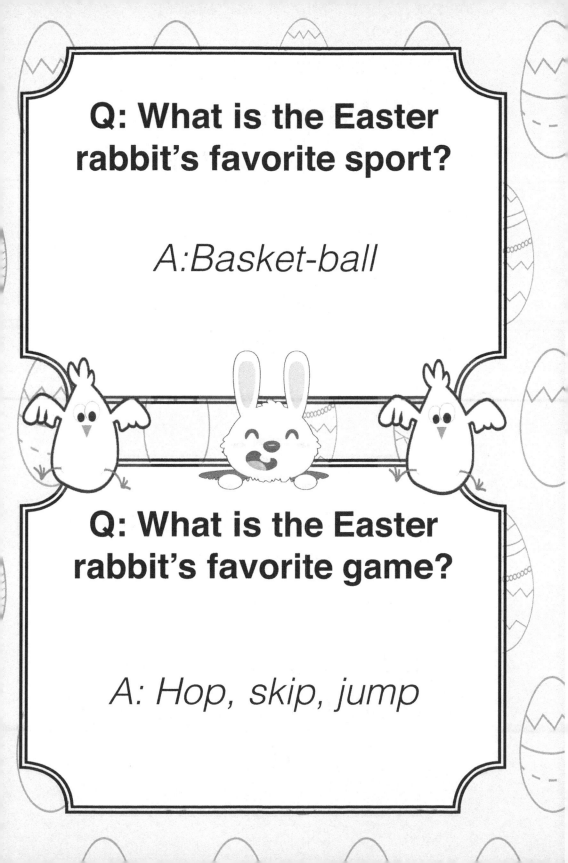

Q: What is the Easter rabbit's favorite game?

A: Hop, skip, jump

Q: Why are there no Easter elves?

A: Because they only come out during Christmas

Q: Why is there no Easter pig?

A: He would eat all of the eggs before you go them

Q: What's the best way to find all the eggs during Easter?

A: Tell everyone else that the Easter bunny is on holiday

Q: Why can't wolves join in an Easter egg hunt?

A: Because they hunt in packs

Q: What does the Easter bunny use to have shiny and neat fur?

A: Hare-spray

Q: What's the worst thing about Easter?

A: Standing on eggs you didn't find

Q: What type of egg comes from outer space?

A: An egg- straterrestrial

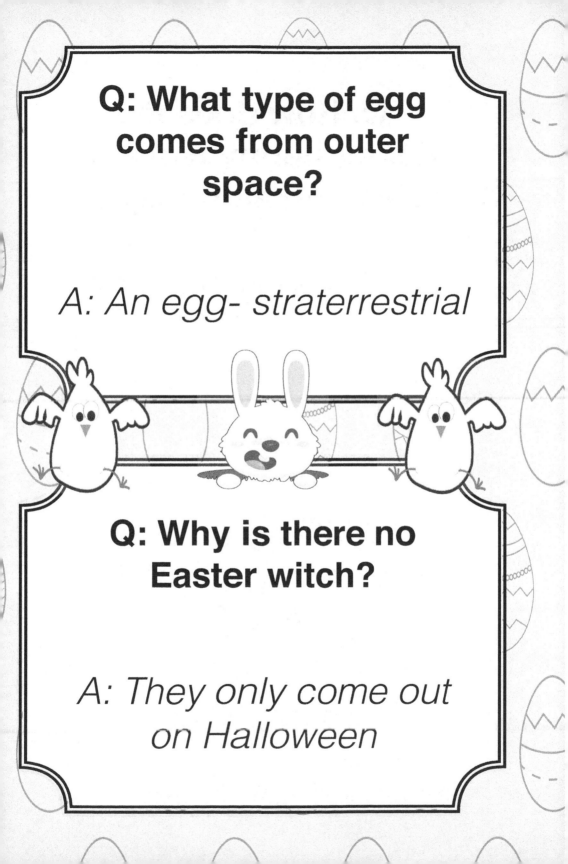

Q: Why is there no Easter witch?

A: They only come out on Halloween

Q: How does the Easter bunny feel after delivering all the eggs?

A: He's eggs-huasted.

Q: What day do Easter eggs worry about the most?

A: Fry-day

Q: What do you call a very naughty egg?

A: A practical yolker

Q: Did you hear about the Easter rabbit secret?

A: No bunny knows

Q: How can you catch the Easter bunny?

A: Dress like a carrot

Q: What's the best way to make Easter easier?

Swap the "t" with an "i

Q: How do you annoy the Easter bunny?

A:Egg-nore him

Q: Why did the Easter egg run faster than the other eggs?

A: It was afraid of being eaten

Q: What crime does the Easter egg hate the most?

A: Poaching

Q: How does the Easter bunny make an egg roll?

A: With a little push of course

Q: What happened to the boy who found all the Easter eggs?

A: He was said to be egg-static

Q: How does the Easter bunny leave its home?

A: Through the eggs-it (exit)

Q: Did you hear about the scared Easter eggs?

A: They were terr-fried

Q: Did you hear about the funny Easter egg?

A: He came from a comedi-hen

Q: Why did the Easter egg turn up early for school?

A: He had an eggs-am

Q: Why was the Easter egg a terrible driver?

A: He eggs-celerated too much

Q: What do you call an adventurous Easter bunny in the jungle?

A: An eggs-plorer

Q: Why did the Easter egg hide from the cook?

A: He didn't want to whisk being caught

Q: What did the Easter bunny order at the coffee shop?

A: An eggs-presso

Q: Why did the Easter bunny not hide the eggs?

A: They were free range

Q: Who is the Easter bunny's favorite singer?

A: Egg Sheeran

Q: How do you know if the Easter bunny is real?

A: Well, can you imagine a person being silly enough to dress up as one?

Q: Why are there no Easter Ostriches?

A: Have you seen the size of their eggs, they would be hard to hide.

Q: What should you paint on an egg?

A: Your name so nobody can steal it

Q: What's the Easter bunny's favorite movie?

A: Peter Rabbit

Q: How do you make the Easter bunny sad?

A: Hide all the eggs before he does

Q: What does the Easter bunny eat for dinner?

A: Carrots, he is a rabbit

Q: Where's the last place you would want to find an Easter egg?

A: In the toilet

Q: Why is the Easter bunny always hopping around?

A: If he walked, he might step on an egg

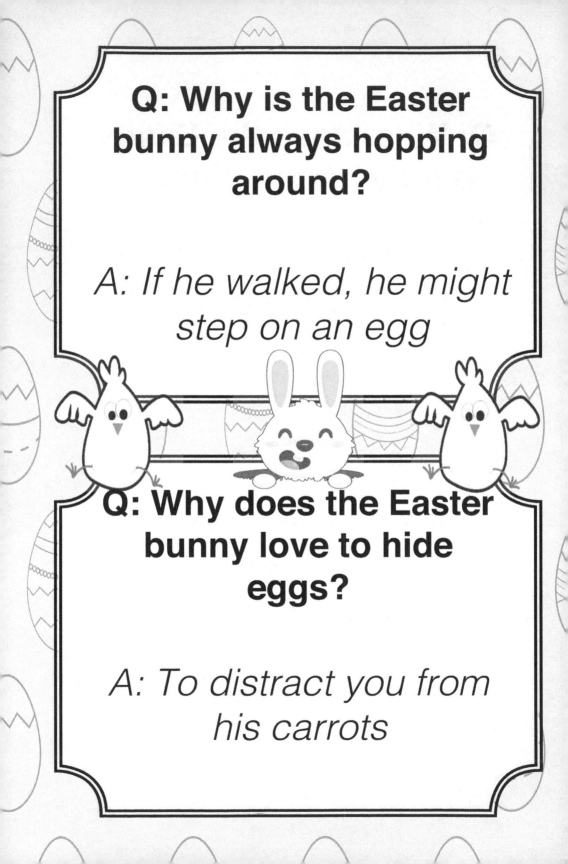

Q: Why does the Easter bunny love to hide eggs?

A: To distract you from his carrots

Q: What did the Easter bunny say when his friend stop talking to him?

A: Are you egg-noring me?

Q: Why does the Easter bunny carry a basket?

A: Because he had eggs in there silly

Q: How do you get the Easter bunny to show you where he hides all the eggs?

A: Give him a big bunch of carrots

Q: Where does the Easter rabbit hide eggs if he doesn't like you?

A: In your shoes

Q: Where does the Easter rabbit hide eggs if he does like you?

A: In your pockets

Q: Where does the Easter rabbit hide eggs if he wants you to eat healthy?

A: In a fruit bowl

Q: Where does the Easter rabbit hide eggs if he wants you to get exercise?

A: On a trampoline

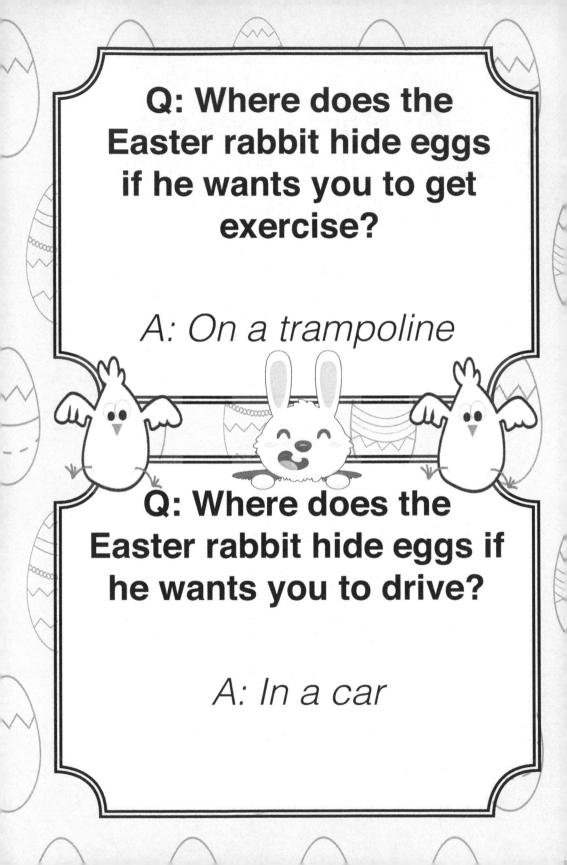

Q: Where does the Easter rabbit hide eggs if he wants you to drive?

A: In a car

Q: Where does the Easter rabbit hide eggs if he wants you to read?

A: In a library

Q: Where does the Easter rabbit hide eggs if he wants you to swim?

A: In a pool

Q: Where does the Easter rabbit hide eggs if he wants you to go to the beach?

A: In a sand bucket

Q: Where does the Easter rabbit hide eggs if he wants you to tidy your room?

A: He gives them to your parents to hide